I0455301

Biography of Mahommah G. Baquaqua, a Native of Zoogoo, in the Interior of Africa.

(A Convert to Christianity,) With a Description of That Part of the World; Including the Manners and Customs of the Inhabitants, Their Religious Notions, Form of Government, Laws, Appearance of the Country, Buildings, Agriculture, Manufactures, Shepherds and Herdsmen, Domestic Animals, Marriage Ceremonials, Funeral Services, Styles of Dress, Trade and Commerce, Modes of Warfare, System of Slavery, &c., &c. Mahommah's Early Life, His Education, His Capture and Slavery in Western Africa and Brazil, His Escape to the United States, from Thence to Hayti, (the City of Port Au Prince,) His Reception by the Baptist Missionary There, The Rev. W. L. Judd; His Conversion to Christianity, Baptism, and Return to This Country, His Views, Objects and Aim. Written and Revised from His Own Words, by Samuel Moore, Esq., Late Publisher of the "North of England Shipping Gazette," Author of Several Popular Works, and Editor of Sundry Reform Papers

Mahommah Gardo Baquaqua

Samuel Moore

DETROIT:
Printed for the Author, Mahommah Gardo
Baquaqua,
BY GEO. E. POMEROY & CO., TRIBUNE
OFFICE.
©1854.

NUMBERS.

- Afo, one.
- Ahinka, two.
- Ahiza, three.
- Attoche, four.
- Ahgo, five.
- Aido, six.
- Aea, seven.
- Aeako, eight.
- Aega, nine.
- Away, ten.
- Awaychinefaw, eleven.
- Awaychineka, twelve.
- Awaychineza, thirteen.
- Awaychinetache, fourteen.
- Awaychinago, fifteen.
- Awaychinedo, sixteen.
- Awaychinea, seventeen.
- Awaychineako, eighteen.
- Awaychinego, nineteen.
- Awarranka, twenty.
- Awarrankachnefaw, twenty-one
- Awarrankachineka, twenty-two
- Awarrankachnega, twenty-three
- Awarrankachintache, twenty-four.
- Awarrankachinego, twenty-five
- Awarrankachinedo, twenty-six.
- Awarrankachinea, twenty-seven.
- Awarrankachineake, twenty-eight.
- Awarrankachinega, twenty-nine.
- Awarranza, thirty.
- Awarranzachinefaw, thirty-one

5

- Awarranzachineka, thirty-two.
- Awarranzachineza, thirty-three
- Awarranzachintoche, thirty-four.
- Awarranzachinego, thirty-five.
- Awarranzachinedo, thirty-six.
- Awarranzachinea, thirty-seven
- Awarranzachineako, thirty-eight.
- Awarranzachinega, thirty-nine.
- Waytoche, forty.
- Waytochechinefaw, forty-one.
- Waytochechineka, forty-two.
- Waytochechineza, forty-three.
- Waytochechintoche, forty-four
- Waytochechinego, forty-five.
- Waytochechinedo, forty-six.
- Waytochechinea, forty-seven.
- Waytochechineaka, forty-eight
- Waytochechinega, forty-nine.
- Waygodada, fifty.
- Waygochinefaw, fifty-one.
- Waygochineka, fifty-two.
- Waygochineza, fifty-three.
- Waygochintoche, fifty-four.
- Waygochinego, fifty-five.
- Waygochinedo, fifty-six.
- Waygochinea, fifty-seven.
- Waygochineako, fifty-eight.
- Waychinaga, fifty-nine.
- Waydo, sixty.
- Waydochinefaw, sixty-one.
- Waydochineka, sixty-two.
- Waydochineza, sixty-three.
- Waydochintoche, sixty-four.

- Waydochinego, sixty-five.
- Waydochinedo, sixty-six.
- Waydochinea, sixty-seven.
- Waydochineako, sixty-eight.
- Waydochinega, sixty-nine.
- Wayea, seventy.
- Wayeachinefaw, seventy-one.
- Wayeachineka, seventy-two.
- Wayeachineza, seventy-three.
- Wayeachintoche, seventy-four.
- Wayeachinego, seventy-five.
- Wayeachinedo, seventy-six.
- Wayeachinea, seventy-seven.
- Wayeachineako, seventy-eight.
- Wayeachinega, seventy-nine.
- Wako, eighty.
- Waykochinefaw, eighty-one.
- Wakochineka, eighty-two.
- Wakochineza, eighty-three.
- Wakochintoche, eighty-four.
- Wakochinego, eighty-five.
- Wakochinedo, eighty-six.
- Wakochinea, eighty-seven.
- Wakochineako, eighty-eight.
- Wakochinega, eighty-nine.
- Wayga, ninety.
- Waygachinefaw, ninety-one.
- Waygachineka, ninety-two.
- Waygachineza, ninety-three.
- Waygachintoche, ninety-four.
- Waygachinego, ninety-five.
- Waygachinedo, ninety-six.
- Waygachinea, ninety-seven.

- Waygachineako, ninety-eight.
- Waygachinega, ninety-nine.
- Zongfawdaday, one hundred.
- Zongeka, two hundred.
- Zongeza, three hundred.
- Zongtoche, four hundred.
- Zonggo, five hundred.
- Zongedo, six hundred.
- Zongea, seven hundred.
- Zongeako, eight hundred.
- Zongega, nine hundred.
- Zongway, one thousand.

PREFACE AND COMPILER'S NOTES.

IN compiling the following pages, many difficulties have had naturally to be encountered, in consequence of the imperfect English spoken by Mahommah, but great care has been taken to render the work as readable and clear as possible to the capacities of all classes of readers; the description of the people (their manners and customs) of that country, which is so little known to the world at large, will be found highly instructive--the friends of the poor African negro and the colored race generally, will be greatly benefitted by reading the work carefully from beginning to end; they will there see throughout its pages, the horrible sufferings and tortures inflicted upon that portion of God's creatures, merely because "their skin is of a darker hue," notwithstanding their hearts are as soft and flexible as the man of paler cast. The cherished object of Mahommah has been for a long time past, indeed ever since his conversion to christianity whilst at Hayti, to be enabled to return again to his native land, to instruct his own people in the ways of the gospel of Christ, and to be the means of their salvation, which it is to be hoped he will be able to accomplish ere long; in the meantime he has become a subject of the Queen of England, and is at present living under her benign laws and influence in Canada. stirring up the colored population and agitating for the abolition of slavery all over the world, a cause which ought to occupy the hearts and feelings of every benevolent and charitable man and woman throughout the world; the slaves

themselves, it is to be hoped, will be benefitted by
every line that is written in their favor, simple as the
style may be; as their cause is the cause of suffering
humanity, how can any one boasting of the religion
of Jesus Christ, for one moment seek to uphold
slavery as it is for a single day? No, it cannot be; the
system of slavery and the doctrines of Christ are
quite opposed to each other; no matter what the
defenders of the system may say! Readers, judge for
yourselves, and act for yourselves; depend not on
the dogmas of any man or class of men, but read,
mark, learn and inwardly digest the subject matter
of these pages, and compare the treatment of those
poor creatures under the yoke of slavery, and the
gospel of Christ, and you will soon come to the
conclusion, that it will not bear comparison with
any one portion of the good book, which says "my
yoke is easy and my burden is light"--for the yoke
of slavery is hard and the burdens are not light, but
exceedingly heavy.

Too much cannot be said, written or published,
on the horrible system of slavery. To bring the
brutal subject to an end, the more that is said and
done in the way of agitating the subject, the better
for all classes, the better for slave owners, to get rid
of the "accursed sin," and the better for the poor
slaves to rid them of their yoke; let all whose hearts
are not of adamant and whose nerves are not of
steel, advance his views in every possible way and
the slave may soon become free, and bless the day
that made him so, and the hands that knocked the
shackles from his bleeding hands and feet, and

snatched the whip from out the tyrant master's hand, who bound up all the negro's wounds and applied balm to his writhing body. Can the humane and philanthropic who struggled for the freedom of the slaves in the West India possessions some years ago, and which cost the British people, some millions of pounds sterling,--I say can they forget the pleasurable feelings that event gave to them. The Society of Friends were the principal agitators in that movement, and the blessings and prayers of the poor liberated slaves ascended the altars of heaven on that great occasion; can they forget the kindlier feelings of their nature that was stirred up within them on that occasion, can they ever, think you, forget the glorious day which made their fellow creatures free; can they forget the first of August of that eventful year? Oh then, friends of humanity, bestir yourselves again, as did those good men on that occasion, and persevere until you have accomplished the work you have set yourselves to do, as those in days gone by had done.

This little work may have its desired effect wherever it is read, and no doubt the sufferings of the subject (Mahommah) will bring the tear to many a pitying eye, and the blush to many a dimpled cheek, in shame for the cruelty practised upon him by men bearing the image of their Maker, many a blush will be summoned to the cheeks of innocence whilst this work is in progress of perusal.

The descriptive part of this work cannot but prove highly interesting to the general reader, as such descriptions coming from the mouth of a native who has passed through all the places described, in the interior of a country like Africa. Many works descriptive of the country have issued from the press from time to time, but none have appeared like the present; it is simply a compilation or narration of events happening in the life of the man himself who narrates them, and given without any figured speech, but in the plainest style possible; all the phrases used are "familiar as household words." consequently it will be easily understood by all who read it; it is written so plainly in point of speech, that "he who runs may read." The different customs and ceremonies are very amusing, and may, according to the way in which it is read, prove highly instructive, as well. It is hoped that, at any rate, good may be accomplished by its publication. If it should be the province of Mahommah to go out to Africa as a missionary, according to his heart's desire, it is his intention, if he is permitted to return to this country, to issue this work in a larger form, with the addition of matters that has either been entirely left out or curtailed for want of space, together with his success amongst his native race, the people of his own clime.

BIOGRAPHY
OF
MAHOMMAH GARDO BAQUAQUA,
&c., &c.
CHAPTER I.

THE subject of this memoir was born in the city of Zoogoo, in Central Africa, whose king was tributary to the king of Bergoo. His age is not known to the year exactly, as the Africans have altogether a different mode of dividing time and reckoning age, but supposes he is about 30 years old, from the remembrance of certain events which took place, and from the knowledge he has lately acquired in figures. But this not being a very important matter in his history, we here leave it to its own obscurity, not for a moment believing the narration will lose any of its interest from the lack of the particular figure.

He states his parents were of different countries, his father being a native of Bergoo, (of Arabian descent) and not very dark complexioned. His mother being a native of Kashna and of very dark complexion, was entirely black. The manners of his father were grave and silent; his religion, Mahomedanism.

As the interior of Africa is comparatively little known, a brief sketch cannot prove but very interesting to most of our readers; accordingly we shall proceed with the details as set forth by

14

Mahommah himself. Their mode of worship is something after the following style:

My father, (says Mahommah) rose every morning at four o'clock for prayers, after which he returned to bed, at sunrise he performed his second devotional exercises, at noon he worshipped again, and again at sunset.

Once a year a great fast is held, which lasts a month, during this time nothing is eaten during the day, but in the evening, after some ceremonies are performed, eating is allowed; after eating, worship is permitted in their own homes, and then assemblies for public worship are held. The place of worship was a large and pleasant yard belonging to my grandfather, my uncle was the officiating priest. The oldest people arrange themselves in rows, the priest standing in front, the oldest people next to him, and so on, arranging themselves in order according to age.

The priest commences the devotions by bowing his head toward the earth and saying the following words: "Allah-hah-koo-bar," the people responding "Allah-hah-koo-bar," signifying "God, hear our prayer, answer our prayer." The priest and people then kneel and press their foreheads to the earth, the priest repeating passages from the Koran, and the people responding as before. After this portion of the ceremony is over, the priest and people sitting on the ground count their beads, the priest occasionally repeating passages from the

Koran.--They then pray for their king, that Allah would help him to conquer his enemies, and that he would preserve the people from famine, from the devouring locusts, and that he would grant them rain in due season.

At the close of each day's ceremonies, the worshippers of the prophet go to their respective homes, where the best of everything is provided for the evening's repast. This same worship is repeated daily for thirty days, and closes with one immense mass meeting. The king comes to the city on this occasion and great multitudes from the country all round about, who together with the citizens, collect at the place appointed for worship, called Gui-ge-rah, a little out of the city. This place consecrated to the worship of the false prophet, is one of "God's first Temples." It consisted of several very large trees, forming an extensive and beautiful shade, the ground sandy and entirely destitute of grass, is kept perfectly clean, many thousands can be comfortably seated beneath those trees, and being upon high ground, the appearance of such a mighty assembly, is imposing in the extreme, the seats are merely mats spread out upon the ground. A mound of sand (this sand difers from the sand of the desert, it is a coarse red sand mixed with earth and small stones and can easily be formed into a substantial mound) is raised for the chief priest to stand upon whilst he addresses the people. On these occasions he is dressed in a loose black robe, reaching nearly to the ground, and is attended by four subordinate priests, who kneel around him, holding the bottom of his

16

robe, waving it to and fro. Occasionally the chief priest will "squat like a toad," and when he arises, they resume the operation of waving his robe. These ceremonies concluded the people return home to offer sacrifice, (sarrah) for the dead and living. Thus ends the annual fast.

CHAPTER II.
Government in Africa.

IN Africa they have no written or printed forms of government, and yet the people are subject to certain laws, rules and regulations. The government is vested in the king as supreme, next to him are chiefs or petty sovereigns, there are also other officers, whose titles and office cannot be explained very well in English.

The king of Zoogoo, as before stated, is tributary or subservient to the king of Bergoo. Theft is considered the greatest crime in some parts of Africa, and the thief frequently receives the punishment of death in consequence. When any one is suspected or charged with theft, he is taken before the king, where a sort of trial is given him; if found guilty, he is either sold or put to death; where the latter sentence is carried into effect, any one is allowed to stone or otherwise abuse and maltreat him, when he is finally led to the top of a small hill in the city and either stoned or shot to death. Murder is not considered so great a crime, and a murderer does not receive capital punishment, but is mostly sold as a slave and sent out of the country.

The crime of adultery is severely punished, but the heaviest punishment is inflicted upon the man; a case in point is thus described by Mahommah, he says: "I remember an individual that was severely punished for this crime. The king's brother had several wives, one of whom was suspected of

18

incontinency. Both were brought before the king--I was with him at the time. The king ordered me to get a rope, which was fastened around the man's arms, behind his back and tied, then a stick was placed in the rope, which had been wetted so as to make it shrink, and then twisted around until the poor creature was forced into a confession of his guilt, when he was released and given away as a slave. The woman received no other punishment than that of witnessing the torture inflicted upon her guilty paramour.

The farmers have their crops secured in this way.--The farms not being fenced in, the king makes a law, that every man who owns a horse, donkey, or other animal, must keep them from his neighbors' promises. If any animal strays upon the neighbors' premises, and does the least damage, he is caught and tied up, and the owner obliged to pay a heavy fine before he can recover the animal. This is the style of impounding in Africa.

Debts are sometimes collected in the following manner, viz:--If a person in one town or city, is indebted to a person residing at a distance and refuses or neglects to pay such a debt, the creditor residing in such distant town or city may seize upon any of his neighbors, whom he may happen to catch in that town, and if he has any money or thing valuable, the creditor is allowed to take it from him, and tell such stranger to get it from his fellow townsman when he returns home again; if he has no property about him, he is allowed to seize upon his person and detain him until the debt is paid. Such a law in this country would have very great effect in keeping the citizens pretty much confined to their own homes, as the danger of traveling would be very great; the chances of return to an anxious and affectionate wife, would in most civilized countries be very small indeed. Supposing the rambler to be destitute of property, and supposing him to be a man of means, there is no doubt of his means being considerably reduced, ere his return to his happy home.

The soldiers are a privileged class, and whatever they need either in town or city, they are allowed to take, and there is no redress, from any complaint made against them. If a slave becomes dissatisfied, he leaves his master and goes to the king, and becomes a soldier, and thereby gains his freedom from his master. No "fugitive slave law" can touch him. These are some of the principal matters which are brought before the king for adjustment, which he disposes of, according to the laws of the land.

CHAPTER III.
Appearance and Situation of the Country

It is rather difficult to give a very correct account of the geography of that part of Africa, described as the birth-place of Mahommah; but it must be situate somewhere between ten and twenty degrees north latitude, and near the meridian of Greenwich. It is situated in the peninsular formed by the great bend of the river Niger.

Up to the time that Mahommah was "forced from home and all its pleasures," the foot of the white man had not made its first impress upon the soil; therefore the facts, matters, and things hereby related, will be the more interesting to all those whose hearts and souls are turned toward the wants and woes of that portion of the globe.

The city of Zoogoo is in the midst of a most fertile and delightful country; the climate, though exceedingly hot, is quite healthy. There are hills and mountains, plains and valleys, and it is pretty well watered. About a mile from the city there is a stream of water, as white as milk and very cool, and not far from that there is a spring of very cold water, also quite white. The residents often go from the city thence for water.

It is not in the midst of a wilderness, as some suppose, but there are some quite extensive plains, covered with very tall rank grass, which is used by the people to cover their houses, after the fashion of

21

thatching. On these plains there are but few trees, but what there are, are of great size. And here also, roams the elephant, the lion, and other wild animals, common to the torrid zone. There are two kinds of elephants, one very large, called Yah-quim-ta-ca-ri, the other small, called Yah-quin-ta-cha-na. The teeth of the elephant lie scattered about in abundance all over the plains, and can be collected in any quantity. The natives use the teeth to make musical instruments, which they call Ka-fa.

The city itself is large, and surrounded by a thick wall, built of red clay and made very smooth on both sides. The outer side of the wall is surrounded by a deep moat or ditch, which in the rainy season is filled with water. Beyond this, the city is further protected by a hedge of thorns, grown so thickly and compactly together that no person could pass through them; it bears a small white blossom, and when in full bloom looks exceedingly beautiful.

The king's palace (if it may be so called) is within the city wall, at some little distance from the principal part of the city, surrounded by (what in some countries would be called) a park, on a most extensive scale, at the back of which is a dense thicket, precluding the necessity of any protecting wall on that side of the royal domain. A broad avenue leads from the city to the king's house, with an extensive market on either side, beautifully shaded with large overhanging trees. The people of America can have no idea of the size and beauty of some of the trees in Africa, particularly in the cities, where they stand a good distance apart, by that means having the best chance of attaining their full growth. There is a tree called the Bon-ton, which grows to a very great height, but the branches do not spread so wide as some others; it is very Beautiful.

The entrance into the city, is through six gates, which bear the names of their respective keepers, something similar to the city of London and most of the old fortified towns in England, and indeed of most parts of the old country. These gate keepers are chosen for their courage and bravery, and are generally persons of rank. It may perhaps, instruct as well as amuse our young friends, who may read this work, to know their names, and on that account we will give them. 1. U-boo-ma-co-fa. 2. Fo-ro-co-fa. 3. Bah-pa-ra-ha-co-fa. 4. Bah-too-loo-co-fa. 5. Bah-la-mon-co-fa. 6. Ajaggo-co-fa. The word cofa means gate, and Bah, means father. Ajagga is the name of a woman whose son was noted for his valor. In times of war, these gates are strongly guarded, hence the necessity of having chosen men of known valor and courage to keep them.

The houses are built of clay, low and without chimneys or windows.

The following description of one of the dwellings will give a pretty accurate idea of the generality of the houses of the city. A dwelling is composed of a number of separate rooms built in a

23

circle, with quite a space between them; within the outer circle is another circle of rooms, according to the size of the family to occupy them. These rooms are all connected by a wall; there is one large or main entrance in front of the others, in which to receive company. Each family is surrounded by their own dwelling, so that when they are in any apartment, they cannot see any other dwelling, or any one passing or repassing. In consequence of this made of building, the city occupies a very large space of ground.

There is a regularly appointed watch to the city, who are paid by the king, he also acting as chief magistrate over the watch.

CHAPTER IV.
Agriculture, Arts, &c.

The agriculture of the country is in but a very rude state; the few implements used are made by the country people, and consist of a large kind of hoe, to dig up the ground, and small ones to plant and dress the corn, or whatever is to be raised. This process of preparing the ground is very laborious and tedious, but the richness of the soil compensates in some degree; for one acre well tilled, will yield an immense crop. Corn is raised, sweet potatoes and Harnee, which very much resembles the American broom corn in appearance, and is there used as an article of food. Harnebee, which is a very fine grain, grows on a very large stalk, and is unlike anything in this country; it is roasted in the ear, and the grain rubbed out with the hands and eaten as the American people do parched corn; it is very good. Rice is raised in large quantities, and of an excellent quality; it is planted in rows, and one planting will serve two or three years, as it will come up of itself without any attention. It grows very luxuriously. Beans are also cultivated. Fruits grow in great abundance and variety, spontaneously. Yams are cultivated and grow to great perfection. Pine Apples grow spontaneously, but are not eaten, as the natives fear they are of a poisonous quality, but that is only fear, from the want of knowing better. Peanuts are plentiful and of good quality; and there is also a great variety of grain and fruits of other kinds; and supposing they had the means of cultivation, the same as they have in more civilized countries, Africa would be capable of supporting within herself an immense population.

The manufactures of Africa are very limited; they consist of farming utensils, cotton cloths and silk. Silk is but little manufactured, but might be much more, as silkworms are to be found in abundance, and might be increased to any extent. The cotton tree there grows very large, and the cotton is of good quality.

The women do the spinning by a very slow process, having to twist the thread with their fingers; the men do the weaving; they weave the cloth in narrow strips, and then sew it together. Women also grind the corn. The process of grinding is this: They take a large stone and fix it in the ground, they then have a smaller one prepared, so that it can be easily handled; it is pecked on one side after the manner of our mill stones; the women then put the grain or whatever they wish to grind on the large stone and take the other and rub the grain until it is fine; if they wish to make it very fine, they take another stone prepared for the purpose, and by patient labor they succeed in making it as fine as the finest American flour. They grind dried yams by pounding them in a mortar and a fine kind of grain called Har-nee, before named, mixed together; of this mixture they make a kind of stiff pudding, and eat it with gravy made of greens and a variety of vegetables, seasoned with pepper and onions. No kind of food is ever eaten without onions.

The Shepherds and Herdsmen of Africa, are a distinct and subordinate class of people, and belong to the government. They have long, straight hair, and are as light complexioned as the inhabitants of southern Europe; they are nearly white; they take care of the flocks and herds, supply the city with milk, butter and cheese, (the butter is quite good and hard, which is an evidence of its being cooler in this locality than in most other parts of the torrid zone.) They are Mahomedans in their religion, and strictly adhere to the rites and ceremonies of that class of religionists. They speak the Arabic and Flanne languages, hence it must be inferred that they are of Arabian descent, but of their further history, we are in ignorance.

The Domestic Animals of Africa, are much the same as in this and other countries, consisting of the horse, cow, sheep, goat, donkey, mule and ostrich. Birds are abundant, such as geese, turkeys, peacocks; guinea hens and barn fowls; the latter are very large and are in great abundance. They are, together with their eggs, used as the common food for the people in the forests. Besides these, there are abundance of swans in the river, and a variety of wild fowl; there is also a kind of water fowl that is very beautiful, and whose plumage is as white as snow, and about the size of an ordinary dove,--they congregate in large flocks. Parrots are quite common, and singing birds are very numerous.

The rivers abound with the river horse, the crocodile, &c.

CHAPTER V.
Manners, Customs, &c.

Great respect is paid to the aged; they never use the prefix mister or mistress, but always some endearing term, such as, when speaking to an aged person, they say Father or Mother, and an equal, they call brother or sister. Children are brought up to be obedient and polite; they are never permitted to contradict or sit in the presence of an aged person, and when they see an elderly person coming, they immediately uncover, and if they have shoes upon their feet, they immediately remove them. They bend their knee to the aged, and the aged in turn bend their knee to them, and request them at once to rise; and in every respect a deference is paid to age. The best seat is reserved for them, and in their places of worship, the place next to the priest is reserved for them. Should not these facts put to shame the manners of the children in this country towards the aged? How painful it is to witness the disrespect shown to grown up people by the rising generation of this country, and in many cases the shameful behavior of children towards even their own parents, and that without a single check of censure or rebuke!

It is here that the great moral regeneration of our land must commence. Children should be early taught to render obedience and respect to their superiors, and they will then be prepared to render to all, equal rights, when they become men and women, and will in turn be prepared to govern well their own households.

The reader will please pardon this digression; it has been made with a view to draw attention more powerfully to the subject, as it is of vital importance to the well-being of any community, that the young should be properly trained "in the way they should go," so that when they grow up they should "not depart from it." And if this contrast in the behavior of the poor African children, with that of those of our own enlightened nation, may be the means of but one step in the march of improvement and reform in this respect, the compiler of these pages will feel amply repaid for the little exertion bestowed upon these few extra lines. This is one good, nay one of the best features of Africa; another is the law of kindness, which everywhere prevails in the mutual intercourse of those of the same ranks; whatever a person has, he freely divides with his neighbor, and no one even enters a house without being invited to eat.

But the same as in more civilized countries, if a person rises to wealth and honor, he is sure to be envied, if not hated; they do not like to see one of their own number rise above them. A person who has always been rich, they esteem more highly. This seems to be pretty well the case all over the world, go where you will, like seems to produce (in cases of this kind) like. We see the very same thing manifest amongst us every day of our lives, here in our very midst, so that it does not appear that we are greatly removed from the benighted African, with all our wisdom and learning, with all our boasted institutions; truly the whole world is a strange compound of "black, white and gray, and the ways of all mankind are turned every way."

Fighting is of very common occurrence, and is by no means considered disgraceful, there is a place in the city where the young men meet together for that purpose; and as elsewhere, there are two parties who never agree; each party occupies different portions of the city, and they meet for personal combat which often ends in a general fight, but they never kill each other.

CHAPTER VI.
Marriage Ceremonies, &c.

When a young man wishes to marry, he selects a choice fruit called Gan-ran, and sends it by his sister or some female friend to the object of his choice; if the fruit is accepted, he understands that he will be fovorably received, and remains at home for about a week before he pays her another visit. After some time spent in visiting and receiving visits, arrangements are made for the marriage ceremony. They do not have a particular day set, and a wedding at the bride's father's, but she is kept ignorant of the time; the arrangements are made by the bridegroom and her parents. At the time appointed, the bridegroom sends a number of young men to the house of her father at night; they remain out of doors very still and send a child in to tell her some one wishes to speak with her. She goes to the door and is immediately surrounded and carried off by the young men, to a place called Nya-wa-qua-foo, where she is kept six days; during this time she remains veiled and has a number of female friends with her, who spend their time in play and amusements. The bridegroom in the meantime confines himself at home and is attended by his young friends, who also spend their time in feasting and merriment until the seventh day.

Whilst they are thus confined, a general invitation is given to the friends of both parties. The invitation is made in this way: It will be said that My-ach-ee and Ah-dee-za-in-qua-hoo-noo-yo-haw-coo-nah, which signifies that the bride and bridegroom are going out to-day. They all meet at some convenient place named for the purpose. The friends of the bridegroom conduct him there, and the friends of the bride, conduct her also; both bride and groom having their heads covered with white cloths. A mat is prepared for them to be seated; the friends advance and salute the bridegroom, at the same time handing him some money. The money is then placed before the couple, who are thus considered man and wife. Money is likewise scattered for the drum king and his company; also for the children of the populace to pick up. After this, they are conducted to the house of the bridegroom. The ceremonies are thus brought to an end. It ought to have been stated that the favor of the lady's father is obtained by presents.

Polygamy is practised to a great extent, and sanctioned by law. A man's property is sometimes estimated by the number of wives he has. Occasionally a poor man has a number of wives, and then they have to support him. When a rich woman marries a poor man (as is sometimes the case) he never has more than one wife. Mahommah's mother was a woman of rank and wealth. His father had been a wealthy man; he was a traveling merchant; carried his merchandize on donkies, and had slaves to accompany him; but by some means he lost the greater part of his property, and at the time of his marriage was comparatively poor; he consequently had but one wife. This is another reason why it is supposed he was of

Arabian birth, as many of the Arabs travel in this way to gain property.

The women in Africa are considered very inferior to the men, and are consequently held in the most degrading subjection. The condition of females is very similar to that in all barbarous nations. They never eat at the same table with the men, or rather in their presence, (they having no tables) but in separate apartments.

When a person dies, they wrap the body in a white cloth, and bury it as soon as possible. After the body is laid out facing the east, the priest is sent for, and a religious ceremony performed, which consist of prayers to Allah for the soul of the departed.

The manner of burying is to dig a place in the ground, several feet deep and ten or twelve feet horizontally, in which they deposit the body and close up the entrance with a large flat stone. Other ceremonies are also performed by the priest over the grave.

Great lamentations are made for the dead, by loud and bitter cries and wailings, which continue for six days. The friends of the departed, shut themselves up for that space of time, holding meetings for prayer every night. The seventh day, a great feast is held and the term of mourning ends, when the family appear as usual.

The Africans are a superstitious race of people, and believe in witchcraft and other supernatural agencies. Bodies of light, something after the manner of Ignus Fatuas, or Will o' the Wisp, are often seen on the hills and high places, which move fitfully about. These phenomena are supposed to be evil spirits; they have a strange appearance from a distance, and with less ignorant people than the Africans, might be taken for a very different object. They are much larger in appearance than the Jack-o'-Lanthorn of Europe, and seem to proceed from the extended arms of a human being.

When they suppose any person is bewitched, they consult their astrologer, who consults the stars, and by that means trace out the supposed witch, which generally happens to be some poor decriped old woman, whom they take and put to death. This practise seems to be very similar to what was formerly practised in the eastern states, in most parts of old England, and indeed generally throughout Europe "in days gone by." Indeed in many parts of old England, in small isolated towns and villages, the same thing is done at the present day. Of course all such notions have their origin in the grossest ignorance, hence the necessity of educating the masses of the people in every part of the world.

There is a class of men called medicine men, whom the people suppose nothing can hurt; these men have the office assigned them of putting to death these supposed witches. They are called

Unbahs and are scattered all about the country; go in a state of nudity; eat swine's flesh, and are considered by the Mahommedans as a very wicked people.

It is customary for the Mahommedans to wear a loose kind of trousers, which are made full at the bottom and are fastened round about the hips by a cord. A loose robe is worn over this, cut in a circular form, open at the centre, sufficiently large to put over the head, and allowed to rest on the shoulders, with loose sleeves, the neck and breast being exposed. The women wear a cloth about two yards square, doubled cornerwise, and tied around the waist, the tie being made at the left side. The king's dress is made in a similar style, but of more costly materials. Children do not wear much clothing.

The trade carried on between Zoogoo and other parts of the country, is done by means of horses and donkies. Salt is brought from a place called Sab-ba. They exchange slaves, cows and ivory for salt. This journey occupies about two months generally. Occasionally European goods are brought from Ashantee, but they are very costly. Most of the articles used are of home make. Earthenware is made out of clay, they have a nice red and white clay, but the articles they make are very coarse, as they know little of that kind of manufacture, indeed hardly of any other.

They have strange notions concerning the white man. Their notions are very vague and dreamy concerning them. They suppose they live in the ocean, and that when the sun goes down, it warms the water, so that the white people cook their food by it. They consider the white people superior to themselves in every respect, and fear to make needles, as they imagine that the white men can look through an instrument and see all that's going on; and they believe the white man is very angry with them for making needles; they fear very much when thus occupied, and would not be seen by the white man at such a time, could they help it, for all the world. When they are busy at needle making, they of course imagine that they are being looked at; of course this arises from the belief that they are wrongfully engaged, and the same as throughout the whole human race, when a supposed wrong is being perpetrated, fear takes possession of the mind. This is but natural to all mankind; they imagine, for making needles, the whites have the power to put out their eyes. On account of such notions prevailing, of course needles are not made to any great extent, but still some are found hardy and daring enough to make them notwithstanding. From whence such nations sprang, we cannot very well explain, but the all-seeing instrument, is no doubt our telescope, which at some time or other has been exhibited likely by seamen, who have traveled in some parts of Africa, and the story circulated by the wonder-mongers of the sable tribe.

Wars in Africa are very frequent, the country being divided into so many divisions or petty kingdoms. The kings are continually quarreling, which quarrels lead to war.

When a king dies, there is no regular successor, but a great many rivals for the kingdom spring up, and he who can achieve his object by power and strength, becomes the succeeding king, thus war settles the question.

Slavery is also another fruitful source of war, the prisoners being sold for slaves. The weapons used, are bows and arrows, guns, and a kind of knife or short sword, of home manufacture. This knife or sword is worn in time of peace as side arms, as well as in time of war. The Africans never go unarmed.--Sometimes great numbers are killed in the wars, but never so many as in European and other countries. Their prisoners are treated very cruelly; they flog and otherwise abuse them, until an opportunity occurs of disposing of them as slaves. They drink considerably before going to battle, in order to strengthen them and instil them with courage and daring; (of course this has no reference to those professing Mahommedanism, as they use no kinds of intoxicating drinks on any occasion.) Sometimes whole cities are destroyed and the country round about laid waste, when famine ensues.

This alas is too often the consequence of war, wherever it is practised, not only in Africa, but in all parts where the bloody strife is engaged in. When the Gospel, with its beauteous truths are fully understood and appreciated by the people generally, peace and good will shall reign supreme, and "wars and rumors of wars," shall be no more forever.

How strange that nations boasting of enlightenment and the power of the glorious Gospel of Christ to govern them, should so engage, "hand to hand and foot to foot" in such scenes of carnage and destruction. How can christian nations so engaged ever think to succeed in their mission of converting the heathen, when their practises at home are so much at variance with the blessed truths set forth in the sacred volume. Let the christian spirit and the spirit of war array themselves in everlasting opposition, and the day is not far distant when the wilderness shall blossom as the rose with flowers, fitted for the garniture of peace and holiness. Christians, and those professing the doctrines of the Gospel, should do all in their power to banish war. Then would their "yoke be easy and their burthen light," and the work of conversion would go rapidly on.

Slavery in Africa.--The greatest source of misery to Africa is her system of slavery, which is carried on to a fearful extent, but domestic slavery in that country is nothing when compared to this; but the trading of slaves is very horrible. Slaves are taken from the interior and hurried to the coast, where they are exchanged for rum and tobacco, or other articles of merchandize. This system of slavery causes much bloodshed and consequent misery. Mahommah was once taken prisoner and sold, but was redeemed by his mother, but more of this in the proper place.

CHAPTER VII.
Mahommah's Early Life, &c.

We shall now proceed at once to the more important portion of the work, describing the early history, life, trials, sufferings and conversion of Mahommah to christianity; his arrival in America; his journey to, and sojourn in Hayti, and return to this country again; his views, objects and aims.

His parents, as before stated, were of different tribes or nations. His father was Mahommedan in religion, but his mother was of no religion at all. He states: "my mother was like a good many christians here, who like to be christians in name, but do not like to worship God much. She liked Mahommedanism very well, but did not care much about the worshipping part of the matter." Mahommedans are much greater worshippers than Christians, and worship with more apparent zeal and devotion.

The family consisted of two sons and three daughters, besides twins that died in infancy. The Africans are very superstitious about twins; they imagine that all twins are more knowing than any other children, and so with respect to the child born next after twins. They are considered to know almost everything, and are held in high esteem. If the twins live, an image of them is made out of a particular wood, one for each of them, and they are taught to feed them, or offer them food whenever they have any; if they die, the one next to them by birth has an image of them made, and it is his duty to feed them, or offer them food. Mahommah was the next born after twins, and these little duties he faithfully performed. It is supposed the image keeps them from harm and preserves them in war. He was consequently highly esteemed on account of his birth; it was supposed he never said anything wrong, and everything be wished was done for him on the instant. This no doubt was the reason his mother so fondly loved him, and was the cause of his youthful recklessness. They never crossed or controlled him, his mother was the only person who dared to even check him; his love for his mother was exceedingly great. His uncle was a very rich man, who was blacksmith to the king, and he wanted Mahommah to learn that trade, but his father destined him for the mosque, intending to bring him up as one of the prophet's faithful followers. For that purpose he was sent to school, but not liking school very much, he went to live with his uncle and learned the art of making needles, knives and all such kinds of things. His father afterwards replaced him at school, but he soon ran away; he did not like the restraint that his brother (the teacher) put upon him. His brother was a staunch Mahommedan and well learned in Arabic.

Mahommah did not progress very well in learning, having a natural dread of it. The manner of teaching is rather different to other countries, the Africans having neither books nor papers, but a board called Wal-la, on which is written a lesson which the pupil is required to learn to read and write before any other is given; when that lesson is learned, the board is cleaned and a new one written.

Scholars are not permitted to be absent without special leave from the teacher; if truant is played, punishment follows. No fees are due until education is completed. School inspection is made in the following manner: A large meeting house, generally a mosque, is selected, whither the pupils repair together with the teachers, who must rend twenty chapters of the Koran, and if the pupil reads the whole twenty chapters, without missing a single word, his education is considered finished and the fees of instruction are immediately paid.

Mahommah's uncle had property in Sal-gar, whither he would repair to buy gold, silver, brass and iron for the purposes of his business. The gold and silver he made into bracelets, for the arms, and ear rings and finger rings, the Africans being very fond of such kinds of ornaments.

The needles in Africa are made by hand, the process is very tedious; in the first place the iron is hardened or converted into something like steel, it is then made into fine wire, by a process of hammering, and cut into suitable lengths as required, when it is again beaten and made sharp at the point by filing, and finally polished by rubbing on a smooth stone with the hand. From this description of needle making, it may be clearly seen how much labor has to be bestowed upon all branches of manufacture, for want of better tools and machinery.

An African bellows deserves some notice. It is said "necessity is the mother of invention;" whoever doubted this fact, let him attentively read the following, and if they deny that position, they surely cannot but say that the invention of the bellows in Africa, certainly had a "father."

The bellows is composed of a goat skin taken off whole, a stick passes through from the neck to the hinder legs, where it is fastened, and by an ingenious contrivance. The legs are moved up and down by hand, an old gun barrel being used for the pipe.

Whilst his uncle was at Sal-gar on business he died, and left his property to Mahommah's mother. He then worked a short time with another relative.

It is laborious work, manufacturing farming implements and tools. Machinery is greatly needed in Africa, the want of which is a great drawback to the manufactures of that country. The iron is of first-rate quality, very much superior to the iron of America. Iron, copper and brass are twisted into rings, which are worn as ornaments about the ancles and arms.

There are hundreds and thousands of men in the world who rejoice to do good, and who are seeking means to employ their time and their talents. To such as these who peruse the pages of this work, the hint here thrown out may not be lost. A wide field of usefulness presents itself in that much neglected part of the world, where men are to be found, who only need the teaching to make good citizens, good mechanics, good farmers, good men and good christians. To those who would direct their efforts in the behalf of such a nation, no doubt remains but that God would bless their works; their deeds would praise them, and millions yet unborn would called them blessed. Go then, ye philanthropists, and christian men and women, to these benighted people, offer them the hand of assistance and raise them to the standard of their fellow-men, and give all the countenance you can to their endeavors to usefulness and goodness, never caring for the scoffs and frowns of a cold and callous world; let your works be of such a nature as all good men will speak well of you, and your own consciences approvingly assent.

Africa is rich in every respect (except in knowledge.) The knowledge of the white man is needed, but not his vices. The religion of the white man is needed, but more of it, more of the spirit of true religion, such as the Bible teaches, "love to God and love to man." Who will go to Africa? Who will carry the Bible there? And who will teach the poor benighted African, the arts and sciences? Who will do all this? Let the reply be prompt, let it be full of life and energy! Let the Savior's command be obeyed. "Go ye out into all the world and preach the gospel." Save all those who are perishing for lack of knowledge, for the lack of that knowledge, you have the power to impart. Hesitate no longer, for now is the time, the accepted time, "the night cometh when no man can work," and the day (our day) is fast waning. Oh, christian friends, up and be doing.

Mahommah's brother was a kind of fortune teller, who when the king was about to go to war, was consulted by him, to know whether the issue of the war would be in his favor or not; this was done by signs and figures made in the sand, and all he predicted, was fully believed would come to pass, so that by his own mysterious power he could either cause the king to wage war or bring the matter to an end.

He at one time went to Bergoo, some distance from the east of us, where he remained two years. A great war was fought during that time and he was taken prisoner, but was released by his mother paying a ransom, when he returned home again. He then went to Da-boy-ya, which was a long way off to the south-west of Zoogoo, beyond a very large river. At that place a great many kinds of articles of European manufacture were to be found, such as glass bottles, glasses, combs, calicos, &c., but the buildings were mostly the same as those at Zoogoo, but the city was not surrounded by walls, as at the latter. Here also the king was at war and invited my brother. The cause of this war, was that a king had died, and a dispute having arisen (as is very often the case) between two brothers, which should be the king; they adopted such means to decide who should succeed, and he who could gather the greatest forces was the successor. The unsuccessful candidate placing himself under the protection of a neighboring king, until he could gather up sufficient forces to enable him successfully to push on the war, and thus wrest the kingdom from his brother.

After Mahommah's brother had been sometime with the king, Mahommah himself went thither, with many others to carry grain, as it had become scarce there on account of the war. It was about seventeen days' journey from Zoogoo, the manner of travel being on foot, with the sacks of grain upon their heads; a rather tedious and unpleasant mode of traveling and transporting merchandize, considering the facilities for such purposes, afforded in America and Europe.

They arrived safely on a Saturday, and heard that war would be waging that day, but it was not resumed until the next. The king was advised by his counsellor to go out and meet the enemy in the woods, but did not do so. He then went to the King's house, and after breakfasting next morning, the guns began to boom away, and the war went on in earnest. Guns were used by them on this occasion, much more than bows and arrows. The war was too hot for the king, when he, together with his counsellor, fled for their lives.

My companions (says Mahommah) and myself ran to the river but could not cross it; we hid ourselves in the tall grass, but the enemy came and found us, and made us all prisoners. I was tied up very tightly; they placed a rope around my neck and took me off with them. We traveled through a wood and came to a place I shall never forget, full of mosquitoes! But they were indeed mosquitoes, none of your small flys, gnats and such like, that people in North America call mosquitoes, but real big hungry fellows, with stings and suckers enough to drain every drop of blood out of a man's body at one draw. They came whim! whim! about our ears, and bite they did, full of wrathful vengeance. I never wish to be in that place again, or any other like it; it was truly horrible.

Whilst traveling through the wood, we met my brother, but neither of us spoke or seemed to know each other; he turned another way without arousing any suspicion; and then went to a place, and procured a person to purchase me. Had it been known who it was, they would have insisted upon a very great price as my ransom, but it was only a small sum that was required for my release. It should have been mentioned that the city was destroyed, the women and children having been sent away.--When the wars come on suddenly, the women and children have no means to escape, but are taken prisoners and sold into slavery.

After my purchase and release, my brother sent me home again with some friends, and on my return home, I paid our king a visit. He was related to my mother. In a few days after, whilst at home, the king sent for me and said he wished me to live with him entirely, so, accordingly, I remained in his house, and he appointed me a Che-re-coo, that is a kind of body guard to the king. I stood only third from the king, Ma-ga-zee and Wa-roo, being the two only in rank above me, next to the king himself. Ma-ga-zee was an old man, and Wa-roo, a youth. I remained with the king day and night, ate and drank with him, and was his messenger in and out of the city.

The king did not reside in the city, but a few miles from it. (The Africans have a curious way of reckoning distances, they carry their burdens upon their heads and proceed until tired, which is called Loch-a-fau, and in English, means one mile!) The king (continues Mahommah) kept nothing from me, but sometimes, when he had very important affairs in hand, he would consult the more experienced Ma-ga-zee.

The kings are called Massa-sa-ba, and govern several places, and, like the Pharoahs of old, all are called Massa-sa-ba. When the king of the city dies, the Massa-sa-bas are called upon to decide who shall succeed him. If war comes upon them, he is found foremost amongst the brave; his residence is generally in a dense thicket, built after the manner of the country, but garnished on the outside with marble. There are two kinds of marble there, one quite white, and the other red; these marbles are pounded to a fine dust, and whilst the mortar which is used in the building of houses is soft, pieces of the marble are taken and pressed into it, in any fantastic shape and figure they fancy, which makes the wall stronger and gives the building, when finished, a pretty, ornamental appearance.

The mortar in which the women grind yams and Harnee into flour, mentioned in a previous part of this work, requires some like notice, as it is very interesting. A number of men go into the forest and select a very large tree of a particular kind which is used for the purpose, cut it down, and cut off a log about four feet long; it is then hollowed out and made very smooth, and when all is ready the king invites a large number of men, who roll it by hand to his house and place it where it is designed to stand. This mortar is generally so large in circumference that ten or fifteen persons may stand around it to work at one time.

Massa-sa-ba was a generous man and given to hospitality-consequently had a great deal of company. They love feasting in Africa as well as in any other part of the world, and when the kings give feasts, everything that the country affords is provided. This makes them very popular with the people.

Mahommah cannot distinctly state how long he lived with the king, but it was a considerable length of time; whilst he was there he became very wicked. But, (says he,) at that time, I scarce knew what wickedness was; the practises of the soldiers and guards, I am now convinced, was very bad indeed, having full power and authority from the king to commit all kinds of depredations they pleased upon the people without fear of his displeasure or punishment. At all times, when they were bent on mischief, or imagined they needed anything, they would pounce upon the people and take from them whatever they chose, as resistance was quite out of the way, and useless, the king's decree being known to all the country round about. These privileges were allowed the soldiery in lieu of pay, so we plundered for a living.

If the king needed palm wine for a feast, or at any other time he would send me: and I would take some of his slaves along with me, and knowing by what road the country people laden with wine would come into the city, I would, with the slaves, hide in the long grass, whilst one of our number would climb a high tree, and be on the look-out, for any one coming. As soon as he would espy a woman with a calabash on her head, (women only carry the wine to market,) he would inform us, and we would instantly surround her and secure the wine. If the wine was good, she lost it; if poor, we would return it to her, as the king never drank bad wine, but with the caution, that she was to tell no one that the guards were in ambush, otherwise we should not be enabled to fall upon others, so that the king would have to go without his wine. In this way, toll is levied upon all who bear wine into town, whenever the king needs it. If one woman does not carry sufficient wine for the king's use, others are served in the same way until sufficient is obtained; other articles are also seized upon whenever the king needs them.

In front of the king's house or palace, was a very large courtyard, beautifully shaded by lofty trees; on one side of this court there were three or four trees, under which a rude throne was built of earth thrown into a heap and covered over with mortar, being joined from tree to tree, which was several feet high, and ascended by steps of the same material. On the throne there was a seat, cushioned, and covered with red leather, made from the skin of the Bah-seh, which was used for no other purpose. On either side, were seats for his two young wives, which was occupied by two of his favorites in their absence. My seat were at the foot of the throne, on the one side of the steps, and that of Wa-roo on the other; beyond was the seat occupied by Ma-ga-zee.

The king would drink in the presence of his wives, but not eat. Whenever he drank, one of his wives or favorites would kneel before him and place her hands under his chin, so as to prevent any of the drink being spilled upon his person. In their absence, that duty devolved upon me. Whenever the king required me for anything, he would say Gar-do-wa. I would reply Sa-bee (a term used only in speaking to the king,) and immediately run towards him, falling on my face before him, in an attitude of the most respectful attention. He would then state what he needed, when I would go at full speed to obey his commands, walking not being permitted when about the king's business.--When he desired anything of Ma-ga-zee, he would call me, to communicate to him his will. Thus was I kept running about from morning till night, while his feasts lasted. It was very hard work to attend upon such a king, I can assure you, kind readers.

At the king's feasts, all the principal personages would assemble and dine with him, those most of consequence would be entertained at the house of Ma-ga-zee, and those next at other houses, so that the guests were scattered all round about. It is the duty of the women to prepare the food, &c.

To give more fully a description of the manners and customs of the people, would no doubt be highly interesting to most of our readers, and it would give us great pleasure to do so, would the limits of the present work admit of it; but at present, we must hope they will be contented and pleased, with what has already been written for them, and it is to be hoped, they will profit by its perusal. At some other time, should the public think fit to patronize these few stray sheets, it may be, that a larger and more extensive volume may be issued by the author of the present work, in which will be given more fully everything within his knowledge of Africa and the Africans.

We will now, at once, turn to the more interesting portion of Mahommah's history, which treats of his capture in Africa and subsequent slavery. We will give the matter in nearly his own words.

It has already been stated, that when any person gives evidence of gaining an eminent position in the country, he is immediately envied, and means are taken to put him out of the way; thus when it was seen that my situation was one of trust and confidence with the king, I was of course soon singled out as a fit object of vengeance by an envious class of my countrymen, decoyed away and sold into slavery. I went to the city one day to see my mother, when I was followed by music (the drum) and called to by name, the drum beating to the measure of a song which had been composed apparently in honor of me, on account of, as I supposed, my elevated position with the king. This pleased me mightily, and I felt highly flattered, and was very liberal, and gave the people money and wine, they singing and gesturing the time. About a mile from my mother's house, where a strong drink called Bah-gee, was made out of the grain Har-nee; thither we repaired; and when I had drank plentifully of Bah-gee, I was quite intoxicated, and they persuaded me to go with them to Zar-ach-o, about one mile from Zoogoo, to visit a strange king that I had never seen before. When we arrived there, the king made much of us all, and a great feast was prepared, and plenty of drink was given to me, indeed all appeared to drink very freely.

In the morning when I arose, I found that I was a prisoner, and my companions were all gone. Oh, horror! I then discovered that I had been betrayed into the hands of my enemies, and sold for a slave. Never shall I forget my feelings on that occasion; the thoughts of my poor mother harrassed me very much, and the loss of my liberty and honorable position with the king, grieved me very sorely. I lamented bitterly my folly in being so easily deceived, and was led to drown all caution in the bowl. Had it not been that my senses had been taken from me, the chance was that I should have escaped their snares, at least for that time.

The man, in whose company I found myself left by my cruel companions, was one, whose employment was to rid the country of all such as myself. The way he secured me, was after the following manner:--He took a limb of a tree that had two prongs, and shaped it so that it would cross the back of my neck, it was then fastened in front with an iron bolt; the stick was about six feet long.

Confined thus, I was marched forward towards the coast, to a place called Ar-oo-zo, which was a large village; there I found some friends, who felt very much about my position, but had no means of helping me. We only stayed there one night, as my master wanted to hurry on, as I had told him I would get away from him and go home. He then took me to a place called Chir-a-chur-ee, there I also had friends, but could not see them, as he kept very close watch over me, and he always stayed at places prepared for the purpose of keeping the slaves in security; there were holes in the walls in which my feet were placed, (a kind of stocks.) He then took me on to a place called Cham-mah, (after passing through many strange places, the names of which I do not recollect) where he sold me. We had then been about four days from home and had traveled very rapidly. I remained only one day, when I was again sold to a woman, who took me to E-fau; she had along with her some young men, into whose charge I was given, but she journeyed with us; we were several days going there; I suffered very much traveling through the woods, and never saw a human being all the journey. There was no regular road, but we had to make our passage as well as we could.

The inhabitants about Cham-mah live chiefly by hunting wild animals, which are there very numerous; I saw many during the two days, but do not know their names in English; the people go nearly naked and are of the rudest description. The country through which we passed after leaving Chir-a-chir-ee, was quite hilly, water abundant and of good quality, the trees are very large; we did not suffer anything from heat on the journey, as the weather was quite cool and pleasant; it would be a healthy and delightful country, were it inhabited by civilized people, and cultivated; the flowers are various and beautiful, the trees, full of birds, large and small, some sing very delightfully. We crossed several large streams of water, which had it not been the dry season, would have been very deep, as it was they were easily forded, being no more than three feet of water in some places. There were great quantities of aquatic birds sporting about; we saw swans in abundance, we tried to kill some, but found it very difficult, as their movements are very quick upon the water; they have a most beautiful appearance when on the wing, the necks and wings extended in the air, they are perfectly white, never fly very high nor far away; their flesh is sweet and good, and considered a great dish. After passing through the woods, we came to a small place, where the woman who had purchased me, had some friends; here I was treated very well, indeed, during the day, but at night I was closely confined, as they were afraid I would make my escape; I could not sleep all night, I was so tightly kept.

After remaining there for the space of two days, we started on our journey again, traveling day after day; the country through which we passed continued quite hilly and mountainous; we passed some very high mountains, which I believe were called the mountains of Kong. The weather all the time continued cool and pleasant, water was found in great abundance, of very excellent quality, the roads, in some places, where the land was level, was quite sandy, but only for short distances together.-- The country was very thinly settled all the way from Cham-mah, the woods along the route are not very extensive, but large tracts of land, covered with a very tall grass. We passed some places where fire had consumed the grass, something after the manner of the prairies of South and South-western North America.

I will here describe the manner of firing grass in Africa. The grass when it has attained a large growth, is a refuge or haunt for the wild animals, abounding in that part of the country, and when it is decided to fire the grass, notice is sent to all people for miles round about, and the hunters come prepared with bows and arrows, who station themselves all around for several miles, and form a large circle; when the fire is applied at one point, it is soon discovered by the party on the opposite, who immediately fires his portion, and so on, all round about until the whole is fired; the fire strikes inward, toward the centre, never spreading outside the circle; the hunters follow up the flames, and being prepared with branches of trees, bearing large leaves, throw them down before them to stand upon, so as to let fly their arrows upon the terrified animals, who flee before the devouring element into the centre of the fire; the hunters of course following up their game around the outside of the burning mass, slaying all before them as they proceed; they are excellent marksmen, and the poor affrighted creatures have very little chance for their lives, at such times; immense numbers are killed, as well as serpents in great quantities.

But to return:--Whilst passing over those places which had been recently burned, our travel was much quicker, not having much of anything to impede our progress, but where the grass stood as a wall on either side of us, we had to travel very cautiously, fearing the wild animals would spring out and fall upon us. The people of America do not know anything about tall grass, such as in Africa; the tall grass of the American prairies is as a child beside a giant, in comparison with the grass of the torrid zone. It grows generally twelve feet high, but sometimes much higher, and nothing can be seen that is ever so near you, it being so thick and stout; closer even than the small groves of timber in this country. At length we arrived at Efau, where I was again sold; the woman seemed sorry to part with me, and gave me a small present on my leaving them. Efau is quite a large place, the houses were of different construction to those in Zoogoo, and had not so good an appearance.

The man to whom I was again sold, was very rich, and had a great number of wives and slaves. I was placed in charge of an old slave; whilst there a great dance was held and I was fearful they were going to kill me, as I had heard they did so in some places, and I fancied the dance was only a preliminary part of the ceremony; at any rate I did not feel at all comfortable about the matter. I was at Efau several weeks and was very well treated during that time; but as I did not like the work assigned me, they saw that I was uneasy, and as they were fearful of losing me, I was locked up every night.

The country around Efau was very mountainous, and from the city the mountains in the distance had a noble appearance.

After leaving Efau, we had no stopping place
until we reached Dohama; we remained in the
woods by night and traveled during the day, as there
were wild beasts in great abundance, and we were
compelled to build up large fires at night to keep
away the ferocious animals, which otherwise would
have fallen upon us and torn us to pieces, we could
hear them howling round about during the night;
there was one around in particular, the people most
dreaded; it was of the form of a cat with a long
body, some were all of a color, others spotted very
beautifully; the eyes of which shone like lustrous
orbs of fire by night, it is there called the Goo-noo. I
presume from the description, it must be what is
here known as the Leopard, as from what I
understand, the description is about the same.

Dohama is about three days journey from Efau,
and is quite a large city; the houses being built
differently to any I had previously seen. The
surrounding country is level and the roads are good;
it is more thickly settled than any other part I had
passed through, though not so well as Zoogoo, the
manners of the people too, were altogether different
to anything I had ever before seen.

I was being conducted through the city, and as
we passed along, we were met by a woman, and my
keeper who was with me immediately took to his
heels and ran back as hard as he could. I stood stock
still, not knowing the meaning of it; he saw I did not
attempt to follow him, or to move one way or
another, and he called to me in the Efau language to

follow him, which I did, he then told me, after we rested, that the woman we had met was the king's wife, and it is a mark of respect to run whenever she is in sight of any of her subjects. There were gates to this city, and a toll was demanded on passing through. I remained there but a short time, but I learned that it was a great place for whisky, and the people were very fond of dancing. At this place I saw oranges for the first time in my life. I was told, whilst there, that the king's house was ornamented on the outside with human skulls, but did not see it. When we arrived here I began to give up all hopes of ever getting back to my home again, but had entertained hopes until this time of being able to make my escape, and by some means or other of once more seeing my native place, but at last, hope gave way; the last ray seemed fading away, and my heart felt sad and weary within me, as I thought of my home, my mother! whom I loved most tenderly, and the thought of never more beholding her, added very much to my perplexities. I felt sad and lonely, wherever I did roam, and my heart sank within me, when I thought of the "old folks at home." Some persons suppose that the African has none of the finer feelings of humanity within his breast, and that the milk of human kindness runs not through his composition; this is an error, an error of the grossest kind; the feelings which animated the whole human race, lives within the sable creatures of the torrid zone, as well as the inhabitants of the temperate and frigid; the same impulses drive them to action, the same feeling of love move within their bosom, the same maternal and paternal affections are there, the same hopes and fears, griefs and joys, indeed all is there as in the rest of mankind; the only difference is their color, and that has been arranged by him who made the world and all that therein is, the heavens, and the waters of the mighty deep, the moon, the sun and stars, the firmament and all that has been made from the beginning until now, therefore why should any despise the works of his hands which has been made and fashioned according to his Almighty power, in the plentitude of his goodness and mercy.

O ye despisers of his works, look ye to yourselves, and take heed; let him who thinks he stands, take heed lest he fall. We then proceeded to Gra-fe, about a day and half's journey; the land we passed was pretty thickly settled and generally well cultivated; but I do not recollect that we passed any streams of water after entering upon this level country. At Gra-fe, I saw the first white man, which you may be sure took my attention very much; the windows in the houses also looked strange, as this was the first time in my life that I had ever seen houses having windows. They took me to a white man's house, where we remained until the morning, when my breakfast was brought in to me, and judge my astonishment to find that the person who brought in my breakfast was an old acquaintance, who came from the same place. He did not exactly know me at first, but when he asked me if my name was Gardo, and I told him it was, the poor fellow was overjoyed and took me by the hands and shook me violently he was so glad to see me; his name was Woo-roo, and had come from Zoogoo, having been enslaved about two years; his friends could never tell what had become of him. He inquired after his friends at Zoogoo, asked me if I had lately come from there, looked at my head and observed that I had the same shave that I had when we were in Zoogoo together; I told him that I had. It may be as well to remark in this place, that in Africa, the nations of the different parts of the country have their different modes of shaving the head and are known from that mark to what part of the country they belong. In Zoogoo, the hair is shaven off each side of the head, and on the top of the head from the forehead to the back part, it is left to grow in three round spots, which is allowed to grow quite long; the spaces between being shaven very close; there is no difficulty to a person acquainted with the different shaves, to know what part any man belongs to.

Woo-roo seemed very anxious that I should remain at Gra-fe, but I was destined for other parts; this town is situated on a large river. After breakfast I was taken down to the river and placed on board a boat; the river was very large and branched off in two different directions, previous to emptying itself into the sea. The boat in which the slaves were placed was large and propelled by oars, although it had sails as well, but the wind not being strong enough, oars were used as well. We were two nights and one day on this river, when we came to a very beautiful place; the name of which I do not remember; we did not remain here very long, but as soon as the slaves were all collected together, and the ship ready to sail, we lost no time in putting to sea. Whilst at this place, the slaves were all put into a pen, and placed with our backs to the fire, and ordered not to look about us, and to insure obedience, a man was placed in front with a whip in his hand ready to strike the first who should dare to disobey orders; another man then went round with a hot iron, and branded us the same as they would the heads of barrels or any other inanimate goods or merchandize.

When all were ready to go aboard, we were chained together, and tied with ropes round about our necks, and were thus drawn down to the sea shore. The ship was lying some distance off. I had never seen a ship before, and my idea of it was, that it was some object of worship of the white man. I imagined that we were all to be slaughtered, and were being led there for that purpose. I felt alarmed for my safety, and despondency had almost taken sole possession of me.

A kind of feast was made ashore that day, and those who rowed the boats were plentifully regaled with whiskey, and the slaves were given rice and other good things in abundance. I was not aware that it was to be my last feast in Africa. I did not know my destiny. Happy for me, that I did not. All I knew was, that I was a slave, chained by the neck, and that I must readily and willingly submit, come what would, which I considered was as much as I had any right to know.

At length, when we reached the beach, and stood on the sand, oh! how I wished that the sand would open and swallow me up. My wretchedness I cannot describe. It was beyond description. The reader may imagine, but anything like an outline of my feelings would fall very short of the mark, indeed. There were slaves brought hither from all parts of the country, and taken on board the ship. The first boat had reached the vessel in safety, notwithstanding the high wind and rough sea; but the last boat that ventured was upset, and all in her but one man were drowned. The number who were lost was about thirty. The man that was saved was very stout, and stood at the head of the boat with a chain in his hand, which he grasped very tightly in order to steady the boat; and when the boat turned over, he was thrown with the rest into the sea, but on rising, by some means under the boat, managed to turn it over, and thus saved himself by springing into her, when she righted. This required great strength, and being a powerful man gave him the advantage over the rest. The next boat that was put to sea, I was placed in; but God saw fit to spare me, perhaps for some good purpose. I was then placed in that most horrible of all places,

THE SLAVE SHIP.

Its horrors, ah! who can describe? None can so truly depict its horrors as the poor unfortunate, miserable wretch that has been confined within its portals. Oh! friends of humanity, pity the poor African, who has been trepanned and sold away from friends and home, and consigned to the hold of a slave ship, to await even more horrors and miseries in a distant land, amongst the religious and benevolent. Yes, even in their very midst; but to the ship! We were thrust into the hold of the vessel in a state of nudity, the males being crammed on one side and the females on the other; the hold was so low that we could not stand up, but were obliged to crouch upon the floor or sit down; day and night were the same to us, sleep being denied as from the confined position of our bodies, and we became desperate through suffering and fatigue.

Oh! the loathsomeness and filth of that horrible place will never be effaced from my memory; nay, as long as memory holds her seat in this distracted brain, will I remember that. My heart even at this day, sickens at the thought of it.

Let those humane individuals, who are in favor of slavery, only allow themselves to take the slave's position in the noisome hold of a slave ship, just for one trip from Africa to America, and without going into the horrors of slavery further than this, if they do not come out thorough-going abolitionists, then I have no more to say in favor of abolition. But I think their views and feelings regarding slavery will be changed in some degree, however; if not, let them continue in the course of slavery, and work out their term in a cotton or rice field, or other plantation, and then if they do not say hold, enough! I think they must be of iron frames, possessing neither hearts nor souls. I imagine there can be but one place more horrible in all creation than the hold of a slave ship, and that place is where slaveholders and their myrmidons are the most likely to find themselves some day, when alas, 'twill be too late, too late, alas!

The only food we had during the voyage was corn soaked and boiled. I cannot tell how long we were thus confined, but it seemed a very long while. We suffered very much for want of water, but was denied all we needed. A pint a day was all that was allowed, and no more; and a great many slaves died upon the passage. There was one poor fellow became so very desperate for want of water, that he attempted to snatch a knife from the white man who brought in the water, when he was taken up on deck and I never knew what became of him. I supposed he was thrown overboard.

When any one of us became refractory, his flesh was cut with a knife, and pepper or vinegar was rubbed in to make him peaceable(!) I suffered, and so did the rest of us, very much from sea sickness at first, but that did not cause our brutal owners any trouble. Our sufferings were our own, we had no one to share our troubles, none to care for us, or even to speak a word of comfort to us. Some were thrown overboard before breath was out of their bodies; when it was thought any would not live, they were got rid of in that way. Only twice during the voyage were we allowed to go on deck to wash ourselves -- once whilst at sea, and again just before going into port.

We arrived at Pernambuco, South America, early in the morning, and the vessel played about during the day, without coming to anchor. All that day we neither ate or drank anything, and we were given to understand that we were to remain perfectly silent, and not make any out-cry, otherwise our lives were in danger. But when "night threw her sable mantle on the earth and sea," the anchor dropped, and we were permitted to go on deck to be viewed and handled by our future masters, who had come aboard from the city. We landed a few miles from the city, at a farmer's house, which was used as a kind of slave market. The farmer had a great many slaves, and I had not been there very long before I saw him use the lash pretty freely on a boy, which made a deep impression on my mind, as of course I imagined that would be my fate ere long, and oh! too soon, alas! were my fears realized.

When I reached the shore, I felt thankful to Providence that I was once more permitted to breathe pure air, the thought of which almost absorbed every other. I cared but little then that I was a slave, having escaped the ship was all I thought about. Some of the slaves on board could talk Portuguese. They had been living on the coast with Portuguese families, and they used to interpret to us. They were not placed in the hold with the rest of us, but come down occasionally to tell us something or other.

These slaves never knew they were to be sent away, until they were placed on board the ship. I remained in this slave market but a day or two, before I was again sold to a slave dealer in the city, who again sold me to a man in the country, who was a baker, and resided not a great distance from Pernambuco.

When a slaver comes in, the news spreads like wild-fire, and down come all those that are interested in the arrival of the vessel with its cargo of living merchandize, who select from the stock those most suited to their different purposes, and purchase the slaves precisely in the same way that oxen or horses would be purchased in a market; but if there are not the kind of slaves in the one cargo, suited to the wants and wishes of the slave buyers, an order is given to the Captain for the particular sorts required, which are furnished to order the next time the ship comes into port. Great numbers make quite a business of this buying and selling human flesh, and do nothing else for a living, depending entirely upon this kind of traffic.

I had contrived whilst on my passage in the slave ship, to gather up a little knowledge of the

Portuguese language, from the men before spoken of, and as my master was a Portuguese I could comprehend what he wanted very well, and gave him to understand that I would do all he needed as well as I was able, upon which he appeared quite satisfied.

His family consisted of himself, wife, two children and a woman who was related to them. He had four other slaves as well as myself. He was a Roman Catholic, and had family worship regularly twice a day, which was something after the following: He had a large clock standing in the entry of the house in which were some images made of clay, which were used in worship. We all had to kneel before them; the family in front, and the slaves behind. We were taught to chant some words which we did not know the meaning of. We also had to make the sign of the cross several times. Whilst worshiping, my master held a whip in his hand, and those who showed signs of inattention or drowsiness, were immediately brought to consciousness by a smart application of the whip. This mostly fell to the lot of the female slave, who would often fall asleep in spite of the images, crossings, and other like pieces of amusement.

I was soon placed at hard labor, such as none but slaves and horses are put to. At the time of this man's purchasing me, he was building a house, and had to fetch building stone from across the river, a considerable distance, and I was compelled to carry them that were so heavy it took three men to raise them upon my head, which burden I was obliged to bear for a quarter of a mile at least, down to where the boat lay. Sometimes the stone would press so hard upon my head that I was obliged to throw it down upon the ground, and then my master would be very angry indeed, and would say the cassoori (dog) had thrown down the stone, when I thought in my heart that he was the worst dog; but it was only a thought, as I dared not give utterance in words.

I soon improved in my knowledge of the Portuguese language whilst here, and was able very shortly to count a hundred. I was then sent out to sell bread for my master, first going round through the town, and then out into the country, and in the evening, after coming home again, sold in the market till nine at night. Being pretty honest and persevering, I generally sold out, but sometimes was not quite so successful, and then the lash was my portion.

My companions in slavery were not quite so steady as I was, being much given to drink, so that they were not so profitable to my master. I took advantage of this, to raise myself in his opinion, by being very attentive and obedient; but it was all the same, do what I would, I found I had a tyrant to serve, nothing seemed to satisfy him, so I took to drinking likewise, then we were all of a sort, bad master, bad slaves.

Things went on worse and worse, and I was very anxious to change masters, so I tried running away, but was soon caught, tied and carried back. I next tried what it would do for me by being unfaithful and indolent; so one day when I was sent out to sell bread as usual, I only sold a small quantity, and the money I took and spent for whiskey, which I drank pretty freely, and went home well drunk, when my master went to count the days, taking in my basket and discovering the state of things, I was beaten very severely. I told him he must not whip me any more, and got quite angry, for the thought came into my head that I would kill him, and afterwards destroy myself. I at last made up my mind to drown myself; I would rather die than live to be a slave. I then ran down to the river and threw myself in, but being seen by some persons who were in a boat, I was rescued from drowning. The tide was low at the time, or their efforts would most likely have been unavailing, and notwithstanding my predetermination, I thanked God that my life had been preserved, and that so wicked a deed had not been consummated. It led me seriously to reflect that "God moves in a mysterious way," and that all his acts are acts of kindness and mercy.

I was then but a poor heathen, almost as ignorant as a Hottentot, and had not learned the true God, nor any of his divine commandments. Yet ignorant and slave as I was, slavery I loathed, principally as I suppose, because I was its victim. After this and attempt upon my life, I was taken to my master's house, who tied my hands behind me, and placed my feet together and whipped me most unmercifully, and beat me about the head and face with a heavy stick, then shook me by the neck, and struck my head against the door posts, which cut and bruised me about the temples, the scars from which savage treatment are visible at this time, and will remain so as long as I live.

After all this cruelty he took me to the city, and sold me to a dealer, where he had taken me once before, but his friends advised him then not to part with me, as they considered it more to his advantage to keep me as I was a profitable slave. I have not related a tithe of the cruel suffering which I endured whilst in the service of this wretch in human form. The limits of the present work will not allow more than a hasty glance at the different scenes which took place in my brief career. I could tell more than would be pleasant for "ears polite," and could not possibly do any good. I could relate occurrences which would "freeze thy young blood, harrow up thy soul, and make each particular hair to stand on end like quills upon the fretful porcupine;" and yet it would be but a repetition of the thousand and one oft told tales of the horrors of the cruel system of slavery.

The man to whom I was again sold was very cruel indeed. He bought two females at the time he bought me; one of them was a very beautiful girl, and he treated her with shocking barbarity.

After a few weeks he shipped me off to Rio Janeiro, where I remained two weeks previous to being again sold. There was a colored man there who wanted to buy me, but for some reason or other he did not complete the purchase. I merely mention this fact to illustrate that slaveholding is generated in power, and any one having the means of buying his fellow creature with the paltry dross, can become a slave owner, no matter his color, his creed or country, and that the colored man would as soon enslave his fellow man as the white man, had he the power.

I was at length sold to a Captain of a vessel who was what may be termed "a hard case." He invited me to go and see his Senora, (wife.) I made my best bow to her, and was soon installed into my new office, that of scouring the brass work about the ship, cleaning the knives and forks, and doing other little matters necessary to be done about the cabin. I did not at first like my situation; but as I got acquainted with the crew and the rest of the slaves, I got along pretty well. In a short time I was promoted to the office of under-steward. The steward provided for the table, and I carried the provisions to the cook and waited at table; being pretty smart, they gave me plenty to do. A short time after, the captain and steward disagreed, and he gave up his stewardship, when the keys of his office were entrusted to me. I did all in my power to please my master, the captain, and he in return placed confidence in me. The captain's lady was anything but a good woman; she had a most wretched temper. The captain had carried her off from St. Catharine's, just as she was on the point of getting married, and I believe was never married to her. She often got me into disgrace with my master, and then a whipping was sure to follow. She would at one time do all she could to get me a flogging, and at other times she would interfere and prevent it, just as she was in the humor. She was a strange compound of humanity and brutality. She always went to sea with the captain.

Our first voyage was to Rio Grande; the voyage itself was pleasant enough had I not suffered with sea sickness. The harbor at Rio Grande is rather shallow, and on entering we struck the ground, as it happened at low water, and we had great difficulty in getting her to float again. We finally succeeded, and exchanged our cargo for dried meat. We then went to Rio Janeiro and soon succeeded in disposing of the cargo. We then steered for St. Catharines to obtain Farina, a kind of breadstuff used mostly by the slaves. From thence, returned again in Rio Grande and exchanged our cargo for whale oil and put out again to sea, and stood for Rio Janeiro. The vessel being very heavily laden, we had a very bad time of it; we all expected that we should be lost, but by lightening the ship of part of her cargo, which we did by throwing overboard a quantity, the ship and all hands were once more saved from the devouring jaws of the destructive element. Head winds were prevalent, and although within sight of port for several days, we could not make the harbor, do all we could.

Whilst in the doubtful position of whether we should be lost or not, it occurred to me that death would be but a release from my slavery, and on that account rather welcome than otherwise. Indeed I hardly dared to care either way. I was but a slave, and I felt myself to be one without hope or prospects of freedom, without friends or liberty. I had no hopes in this world and knew nothing of the next; all was gloom, all was fear. The present and the future were as one, no dividing mark, all Toil! Toil!! Cruelty! Cruelty!! No end but death to all my woes. I was not a Christian then; I knew not of a Savior's love, I knew nothing of his saving grace, of his love for poor lost sinners, of his mission of peace and good will to all men, nor had I heard of that good land so beautifully spoken of by the poet, "a land of pure delight where saints immortal dwell," and to which land of promise the Christian is daily shortening the journey. No! These "tidings of great joy" had not then been imparted to my gloomy mind, and all was black despair. But when I heard the Savior's words "come unto me all ye that are heavy laden and I will give you rest." I sought and found him, which came as a balm to my wounds, as consolation to my afflicted soul. When think of all this and consider the past, I am content to struggle on in this world to fulfil my mission here and to do the work that is given me to do. Oh! Christianity thou soother of man's sufferings, thou guide to the blind, and strength to the weak, go thou on thy mission, speak the peaceful tidings of salvation all around and make glad the heart of man, "then shall the wilderness be glad and blossom as the rose." Then will slavery with all its horrors ultimately come to an end, for none possessing thy power and under thy influence can perpetuate a calling so utterly at variance with, and repugnant to all thy doctrines.

After great labor and toil we were landed in perfect safety. During this voyage I endured more corporeal punishment than ever I did my life. The mate, a perfect brute of a fellow, ordered me one day to wash down the vessel, and after I had finished, he pointed to a place where he said was a spot, and with an oath ordered me to scrub it over again, and I did so, but not being in the best of humor he required it to be done a third time, and so on again.

When finding it was only out of caprice and there being no spot to clean. I in the end refused to scrub any more, when he took a broom stick to me, and having a scrubbing brush in my hand I lifted it to him. The master saw all that was going on, and was very angry at me for attempting to strike the mate.--He ordered one of the hands to cut a piece of rope for him; he told me I was to be whipped, and I answered "very well," but kept on with my work with an eye continually turned towards him, watching his movements. When I had set the breakfast ready, he came behind me before I could get out of his way, and struck me with the rope over my shoulders, and being rather long, the end of it swung down and struck my stomach very violently, which caused me some pain and sickness; the force with which the blow was struck completely knocked me down and afterwards he beat me whilst on deck in a most brutal manner.--My mistress interfered at this time and saved me from further violence.

We remained at Rio Janeiro nearly a month. Whilst there an incident occurred, which I will relate in illustration of the slave system.

One day it was necessary for me to go ashore with my master as one of the oarsmen, and whilst there I drank pretty freely of wine, and seeing my master about returning to the boat I made for where it lay, and being rather confused with drink as well as flurried at seeing my master, I fell into the water, but it being only shallow, I suffered nothing further than a good ducking for my drunkenness. I was easily got out. Whilst rowing my master, my head swam very much from the effects of the liquor I had drank, and consequently did not pull very steadily, when my master seeing the plight I was in asked me what was the matter, I said "nothing sir;" he said again, "have you been drinking?" I answered no sir! So that by being ill used I learned to drink, and from that I learned to tell lies, and no doubt should have gone on step by step from bad to worse, until nothing would have been wicked enough for me to have done, and all this through the horrible system of slavery. But I am happy to say that through the grace of God, I was led to abandon my evil ways.

When the cargo was landed, an English merchant having a quantity of coffee for shipment to New York, my master was engaged for the purpose, and it was arranged, after some time that I should accompany him, together with several others to serve on ship board.

We all had learned, that at New York there was no slavery; that it was a free country and that if we once got there we had nothing to dread from our cruel slave masters, and we were all most anxious to get there.

Previous to the time of the ship's sailing, we were informed that we were going to a land of freedom. I said then you will never see me any more after I once get there. I was overjoyed at the idea of going to a free country, and a ray of hope dawned upon me, that the day was not far distant when I should be a free man. Indeed I felt myself already free! How beautifully the sun shone on that eventful morning, the morning of our departure for that land of freedom we had heard so much about. The winds too were favorable, and soon the canvass spread before the exhilerating breeze, and our ship stood for that happy land. The duties of office, on that voyage, appeared light to me indeed, in anticipation of seeing the goodly land, and nothing at all appeared a trouble to me. I obeyed all orders cheerfully and with alacrity.

That was that the happiest time in my life, even now my heart thrills with joyous delight when I think of that voyage, and believe that the God of all mercies ordered all for my good; how thankful was I.

The winds held favorable for a speedy passage several days together, after which we experienced very rough, tempestuous weather, which somewhat retarded our progress, and put us in some danger of being sent "to that bourne from whence no traveler returns," as fears were entertained for our safety. One night during the voyage, it blew a perfect hurricane the whole night, and just previous to day-break, the lamps in the binnacle went out with the heavy rolling of the ship. I was ordered to light it, but on account of the high wind, after several attempts I entirely failed. Aha, says the captain, my boy you can't light the binnacle, can't you?

The man at the helm said it was light enough, he could do without it, he could see the compass well enough; but as orders were given, whether the light was wanted or not, they must be obeyed; so three other hands were called and a blanket was placed around the binnacle to keep off the wind, when they succeeded at length in lighting it, but I not understanding how to do it, could not light it; I had tried over and over again. After this the captain got out of his berth, dressed himself and ordered me to light his lamp; when I went to him he took a large stick for the purpose of striking me, and aiming a blow at my head, I raised my arm to prevent my head being struck, he told me to keep my hand down. I did so, but when the blow was falling I again raised my hand and succeeded in saving my skull from being cracked; he did not want to strike my hand as that would provent me from doing my work, but whether my head was broke or not, I should have had to do my usual work. He then told me to turn round so that he might be able to strike my back. I told him to strike me all that he wanted. He was very angry and struck me at random over my head and body, just where it might happen. I defied him to do his worst, to do what he could and wreak his vengeance fully upon a miserable being like myself. He then called to three of the hands and ordered them to tie me to the cannon. I had thonghts of springing into the water, but was not quite satisfied to go alone; if I could have had the pleasure of taking him along with me I should have willingly done so. The three men fastened hold upon me and placed me upon the cannon, face downwards; they were then ordered to whip me, which they did pretty smartly; he then required me to make submission and beg for mercy, but that I would not do. I told him to kill me if he pleased, but for mercy at his hands I would not cry! I also told him that when they untied me from the cannon, he must take care of himself that day, as when I looked upon my lacerated bleeding body, I reflected that though it was bruised and torn, my heart was not subdued.

As soon as I was loosened I made towards the captain, who gave orders to the men to place me securely in the bow of the vessel and not allow me to go near him again. I was so sore from my bruises and cuts that I could not do anything for several days.

The captain during my sickness would send me good victuals from his own table, no doubt to conciliate me after the cruel wrongs he had inflicted on me, but that was in vain. I was not in any great hurry to get to work again, as he frequently, previous to this, caused me to be flogged for not doing what it would have taken any three men to have done, so that I now felt inclined that he should do without any further services altogether.

Slavery is bad, slavery is wrong. This captain did a great many cruel things which would be horrible to relate; he treated the female slaves with very great cruelty and barbarity; he had it all his own way, there were none to take their part; he was for the time "monarch of all he surveyed;" "king of the floating house," none dared to gainsay his power or to control his will. But the day is coming when his power will be vested in another, and of his stewardship he must render an account; alas what account can he render of the crimes committed upon the writhing bodies of the poor pitiless wretches he had under his charge, when his kingship shall cease and the great account is called for; how shall he answer? And what will be his doom?--That will only be known when the great book is opened. May God pardon him (in his infinite mercy) for the tortures inflicted upon his fellow creatures, although of a different complexion.

The first words of English that my two companions and myself ever learned was F-r-e-e; we were taught it by an Englishman on board, and oh! how many times did I repeat it, over and over again. This same man told me a great deal about New York City, (he could speak Portuguese). He told me how the colored people in New York were all free, and it made me feel very happy, and I longed for the day to come when I should be there. The day at length came, but it was not an easy matter for two boys and a girl, who could only speak one word of English, to make their escape, having, as we supposed, no friends to aid us. But God was our friend, as it proved in the end, and raised up for us many friends in a strange land.

The pilot who came aboard of our vessel treated us very kindly,--he appeared different to any person I had ever seen before, and we took courage from that little circumstance. The next day a great many colored persons came aboard the vessel, who inquired whether we were free. The captain had previously told us not to say that we were slaves, but we heeded not his wish, and he, seeing so many persons coming aboard, began to entertain fears that his property would take in their heads to lift their heels and run away, so he very prudently informed us that New York was no place for us to go about in--that it was a very bad place, and as sure as the people caught us they would kill us. But when we were alone we concluded that we would take the first opportunity and the chance, how we would fare in a free country.

One day when I had helped myself rather freely to wine, I was imprudent enough to say I would not stay aboard any longer; that I would be free. The captain hearing it, called me down below, and he and three others endeavored to confine me, but could not do so; but they ultimately succeeded in confining me in a room in the bow of the vessel. I was there in confinement several days. The man who brought my food would knock at the door, and if I told him to come in he would do so, otherwise he would pass along, and I got no food. I told him on one occasion that I would not remain confined there another day with my life; that out I would get; and there being some pieces of iron in the room, towards night I took hold of one of them--it was a bar, about two feet long--with that I broke open the door, and walked out. The men were all busy at work, and the captain's wife was standing on the deck when I ascended from my prison. I heard them asking one another who had let me ont; but no one could tell. I bowed to the captain's wife, and passed on to the side of the ship. There was a plank from the ship to the shore. I walked across it and ran as if for my life, of course not knowing whither I was going. I was observed during my flight by a watchman who was rather lame, and he undertook to stop me, but I shook him off, and passed on until I got to a store, at the door of which I halted a moment to take breath. They inquired of me what was the matter, but I could not tell them, as I knew nothing of English but the word F-r-e-e. Soon after, the lame watchman and another came up to me. One of them drew a bright star from his pocket and shewed it to me, but I could make nothing of it. I was then taken to the watch-house and locked up all night, when the captain called next morning, paid expenses, and took me back again to the ship along with him. The officers told me I should be a free man, if I chose, but I did not know how to act; so after a little persuasion, the captain induced me to go back with him, as I need not be afraid. This was on a Saturday, and on the following Monday afternoon three carriages drove up and stopped near the vessel. Some gentlemen came aboard from them, and walked about the deck, talking to the captain, telling him that all on board were free, and requesting him to hoist the flag. He blushed a good deal, and said he would not do so; he put himself in a great rage and stormed somewhat considerably. We were afterwards taken in their carriages, accompanied by the captain, to a very handsome building with a splendid portico in front, the entrance to which was ascended by a flight of marble steps, and was surrounded by a neat iron railing having gates at different points, the enclosure being ornamented with trees and shrubs of various kinds; it appeared to me a most beautiful place, as I had never seen anything like it before. I afterwards learned that this building was the City Hall of New York. When we arrived in the large room of the building it was crowded to excess by all kinds of people, and great numbers stood about the doors and steps, and all about the court-yard--some in conversation, others merely idling away the time walking to and fro. The Brazilian Consul was there, and when we were called upon I was asked if we

wished to remain there or go back to Brazil. I
answered for my companion and myself that we did
not wish to return; but the female slave who was
with us said she would return. I have no doubt she
would have preferred staying behind, but seeing the
captain there, she was intimidated and afraid to
speak her mind, and so also, was the man, but I
spoke boldly out that I would rather die than return
into slavery!! After a great many questions had been
asked us, and answered, we were taken to a prison,
as I supposed it was, and there locked up. A few
days afterwards we were taken again to the City
Hall, and asked many more questions. We were
then taken back to our old quarters the prison-
house, I supposed preparatory to being shipped off
again to Brazil, but of that I am not sure, as I could
not understand all the ceremonies of locking us up
and unlocking us, taking us to the court-house to
ask questions and exhibit us before the audience
there assembled--all this was new to me; I,
therefore, could not fully understand the meaning of
all this, but I feared greatly that we were about to be
returned to slavery--I trembled at the thought!
Whilst we were again locked up, some friends who
had interested themselves very much in our behalf,
contrived a means by which the prison-doors were
opened whilst the keeper slept, and we found do
difficulty in passing him, and gaining once more
"the pure air of heaven," and by the assistance of
those dear friends, whom I shall never forget, I was
enabled to reach the city of Boston, in
Massachusetts, and remained there under their
protection about four weeks, when it was arranged

that I should either be sent to England or Hayti, and
I was consulted on the subject to know which I
would prefer, and after considering for some time, I
thought Hayti would be more like the climate of my
own country and would agree better with my health
and feelings. I did not know exactly what sort of a
place England was or perhaps might have preferred
to have gone there, more particularly as I have since
learned that nearly all the English are friends to the
colored man and his race, and that they have done
so much for my people in the way of their welfare
and advancement, and continue to this day to agitate
anti-slavery and every other good cause. As it was, I
determined to go to Hayti; accordingly, a free
passage was procured for us, and considerable
provisions were collected for my use use during the
voyage.

There was on board a colored man of the name
of Jones, who could speak Spanish very well.
During the voyage he took great pains to instruct
me, and to give me correct ideas of things which I
had formed the most absurd notion of. For instance,
a person in walking in the sun will see his shadow;
this shadow I had been led to believe was the soul
of man that I had heard much of, and that when the
body died the soul went to heaven (that is the
shadow), and the body went to earth. His
explanation of this shadow puzzled me very much,
but the solution of the mystery pleased me, and I
began to feel proud of my learning.

I worked occasionally for the captain on our passage to Hayti. When I arrived at Hayti I felt myself free, as indeed I was. No slavery exists there, yet all are people of color who dwell there. I did not know a word of their language, which was Creole; neither did I know where to go or what to do! We, however, went to the Emperor's house first. He was very kind to us. One of the Emperor's Generals, De Pe by name, and a mulatto, gave me plenty to eat and drink, and at night allowed me to lay down with his horses in the stables, and the musquitoes tormented me very much--they teazed me awfully. He often gave me whiskey and brandy to drink, and was every way very kind to me; these favors were (though only trifling in themselves under other circucumstances) to me great indeed, considering what my position was. I went about from house to house "a stranger in a strange land," and without being able to speak one word of the language of the people, and what was worse than all, not a copper in my possession to buy even a loaf to satisfy the cravings of my stomach. At length a colored man from America got me to work for him as cook about his house, but he was a very bad man and I did not stay with him very long. At night he took me up stairs and pointed to the floor where I was to sleep, although there was a bed in one corner of the room, but as soon as his back was turned I got into the bed and slept soundly till morning. When he discovered I had slept in the bed he beat me and knocked me about very much and ordered me not to do the like no more; but the next night I did the same again, for which he shook me about and turned me out of doors. So I became again an outcast and wanderer. I slept in the streets for several nights and became sick, so that when I walked about I was thought to be drunk, as my head was dizzy from the weakness of my system. In this way I went from house to house, and the people could not understand, but thought I was drunk. After this when General De Pe had taken notice of me, as before stated, my fellow in misfortune went to the Baptist Missionary, the Rev. Mr. Judd, and told him our circumstances, stating that we were two slaves from Brazil, and asked him if he could not do something for us, when he agreed to take me into his service, upon which I entered with the most cheerful alacrity.

I remained with him upwards of two years, and a better man or christian than Mr. Judd, in my opinion, cannot be found. He treated me with every kindness; color to him being no cause of ill treatment. Neither shall I ever forget the kindness of his good lady; she behaved to me all the time of my servitude even as a christian should behave. I loved her for her goodness, although at all times I did not behave even to them as they deserved. I must confess, I sometimes treated them rather badly. I had not much gratitude then. I would often get very drunk and be abusive to them, but they overlooked my bad behavior always, and when Mrs. Judd would try to coax me to go home and behave myself, I would fight her and tell her I would not.

After my conversion to christianity I gave up drinking and all other kinds of vices. At the end of that time a stir was made in Hayti to enrol the militia; and being opposed to the spirit of war as well as was my master and mistress, it was agreed that I should leave Hayti on that account, and they provided for me a passage on board a vessel bound to New York, in order to educate me preparatory to going to my own people in Africa, to preach the Gospel of glad tidings of great joy to the ignorant and benighted of my fellow countrymen who are now believers in the false prophet Mahomed.

A book published at Utica, in the State of New York, and entitled "Facts for Baptist Churches," by Mr. A. T. Foss, of New Hampshire, and E. Mathews, of Wisconsin, thus speaks of Mahommah:

"After enduring the yoke for two years in Brazil, he escaped and sought a refuge in this land which boasts of its freedom and philanthropy, but that refuge he sought here in vain. Flying, therefore, from our shores, through a kind Providence, he was conducted to the city of Port au Prince, in Hayti, and to the christian hospitalities of Wm. L. Judd. Our missionary received him gladly, and while he provided him a home and temporal comforts, he failed not to instruct him in the religion of the Gospel. The instruction was to him as life from the dead, and his heart felt its power. He saw and acknowledged its adaptedness to his case as a sinner. He bowed to its authority. He rejoiced in its truth, and became a disciple of its Divine Author."

The baptismal scene, when Mahommah publicly put his trust in Christ, is thus described by Mr. Judd. It is taken from the "Christian Contributor."

"His experience before the Church was was very affecting. Several persons present, not professors of religion, wept on hearing it. He is endowed by nature with a soul so noble that he grasps the whole world at a stroke, in the movements of his benevolent feelings, and the expression of such noble feelings in a style so simple and broken as his, is truly affecting. He now seems filled with the most ardent desire to labor for the salvation of souls--talks much of Africa, and prays ardently that her people may receive the Gospel--dreams often of visiting Kaskua, accompanied by 'a good white man,' as he calls a Missionary, and being kindly received by his mother. He had been asking for baptism a considerable time, when I felt that I could not refuse him any longer. We repaired to the sea side very early in the morning, accompanied by a mixed congregation. After singing and praying in French, I delivered a discourse of perhaps twenty minutes, mostly extemporaneous, upon (Les usages pratiques, de l'ordannance du Bapteme) the practical usages of baptism, founded on Romans vi: 1-4. After this, I prayed in English for the especial benefit of Mahommah.

"In passing down the gentle decent to reach a sufficient depth of water, I asked him if he wished now to devote himself entirely to God and to the good of the world. He replied, 'O yes, Mr. Judd, I want to do all for God, all for good.' In the water of the great deep, which in their eternal freedom rolling, bathe Africa as well as Hayti. I buried him with Christ in baptism, hoping that he may yet be borne upon its surface, as a messenger of mercy to the dark land of his birth."

I will give a slight glance at the voyage from Port au Prince to New York, and relate the incidents connected with it as briefly as possible. We had a most miserable passage, head winds nearly all the way; indeed, they continued from our leaving Hayti until reaching a southern port in the United States of America, into which we were compelled to run on account of the weather. The wife of Mr. Judd accompanied me on my voyage, she being on a visit to the States, where her parents resided.

When the vessel put into port a slave owner came aboard, and seeing me, asked if I was for sale, remarking I was a likely nigger, and would look well skinned, as my hide was a little too dark. We encountered at sea very heavy weather, the ship rocking and pitching most fearfully. We had prayers aboard, but we did not fear the raging of the sea, as our trust was in Him "who resteth the sea, and stilleth the tempest." My mistress was very fond of me, and said she did not feel at all uneasy as long as Mahommah was near her. She had great confidence in me, not that I could have saved her in case of wreck, but I suppose she felt more at rest knowing me, and that I had been about her so long, and served her faithfully.

The weather, however, soon moderated, and we once more set sail again with a fair wind, and was soon on our way to the city of New York again, where we arrived on a Saturday. On the following day, one of the seamen who had professed great friendship for me during the voyage, took it into his head to turn ugly with me. As he was about going ashore, I merely said to him, "give my respects to your wife," as he had been so kind to me. What I said was intended merely as a little civility, when as (I found afterwards) he had been drinking. He took it completely amiss, called me a "nigger," and swore he would give me a thrashing. At night, when he returned again on board, he was very drunk and behaved with great violence, swearing that he would break my head with a stick which he flourished about over my head. I had placed chairs round the table for supper as usual, when he remarked, that he did not intend to sit down with a "nigger." He afterwards got more calm, and sat down and ate like a christian, but this was not till I had let him see a little of my own ugliness, and had threatened to beat him, that he became quieted; when he saw I was no longer to be played with, he gave in, and became a good man, only because he was obliged to.

I followed out the Scripture injunction, to be as "wise as serpents, and harmless as doves," not at all intending to beat him, merely to quiet him. My wisdom I displayed in the first place, not needing to display any other spirit than an harmless one; in the second, I found my "wisdom" sufficient for the case at that time.

We safely reached the shore at New York, and were soon on our way steaming it to Albany, at which place we took the cars to within a short distance of Mrs. Judd's mother's house, which was a little way from a village called Milford in the State of New York. We arrived at Milford early in the following morning, and I was sent on to the house, whilst Mrs. Judd stood at the tavern to fetch a conveyance to take her on. When I reached her mother's house, I had a mind to impress them with the belief that I was a fugitive; but questions being put to me of a positive nature, I could not but give positive answers. I told her I was from Hayti, and she immediately conjectured who I was, as accounts were often sent to her from her daughter in papers printed there, and she asked me if I was Mahommah; I said I was. She wanted to know how I had got to America, who had brought me here. I at once told her, when orders were immediately given for horses, and I returned for my mistress, who was soon once more in the embraces of a kind, good mother. Mother and child had once again met after seas had separated them so great a distance.

I remained there about four weeks, then went to Meredith, in Delaware county, amongst the Free Missions, to see whether they would undertake the task of educating me, when they agreed at once to do so. A gentleman by the name of Dalton was exceedingly kind to me, and undertook my case with the friends of the missions. They then sent me on to McGrawville, at the time C. P. Grosvenor was the President of the College, who was very kind to me, and made much of me, treating me in every way as an equal and a gentleman.

I remained nearly three years in the college, and during that time made very great progress in learning, before leaving the college. My teacher, Miss K. King, composed the following lines, which were spoken by me, before the primary department of the college.

LINES SPOKEN BY MAHOMMAH.

You can't expect one of my race,
With woolly hair and sable face,
And scarce a ray of knowledge
To interest his friends at college.
But, I will do the best I can,
To prove I mean to be a man.
'Tis true, my limbs have fetters
worn,
'Tis true my back the scourge has
borne,
But 'tis not true that tyrant's power
E'er made my heart within me
cower.
No ! that was free as when I played,
Beneath my native palm trees'
shade.

Oh! Africa, my native land,
When shall I see thee, meekly stand,
Beneath the banner of my God,
And governed by His Holy word?

When shall I see the oppressor's rod
Plucked from his hand, my gracious
God?
Oh! when shall I my brethren see,
Enjoy the sweets of LIBERTY?

Friends of the crushed and bleeding
slave,
Ask God to pity! God to save!!
For all the help of man is vain,
Since man for man has forged the
chain.
Oh Righteous Father, thou art just,
To thee I look, to thee I trust;
Oh may thy gracious spirit bear
The Afric's groan, the Afric's prayer,
Up to thy spotless throne above,
Where all is joy and peace and love,
For Jesus' sake, Oh! save the
oppressed,
And let their souls in heaven find
rest.

Whilst at college, some of the young
gentleman there who did not altogether like my
color, played considerable many practical jokes
upon me, and tried to make me some mischief with
the principals. They played all sorts of tricks upon
me; they would, when I was out of the way, scatter
my books and papers all over the room, and pile up
my books in a heap; they would also choko up my
stove pipe with shavings, so that when I attempted
to make a fire, the room would become filled with
smoke; but of these matters, I had only to complain
in the right quarter, and all would be settled. But I
did not like to be continually complaining of them,
so I endured a great deal of their vexatious tricks in
silence. I could not tell why they plagued me thus,

excepting they did not like my color, and that they thought I was a good subject upon which to expend their frolicksome humor.

After I left the college, I went to the Free Missions, with whom I remained a short time, and received more learning from that source. I went to school at Freetown Corner, under the direction of the missions. I lived with my teacher, working occasionally for my board; during my stay here. I had a room to myself, and being cold weather, I always needed a fire, but being no place for the stove pipe to go into a chimney, a lady suggested that I should take a pane of glass from the window and put the pipe through the aperture, which I did, and it answered the purpose very well indeed, until a very windy day came, when the wind blowing down the pipe, caused my room to be filled with smoke; how to remedy the evil, I could not exactly tell, but an ingenious thought struck me. I went to the closet and procured a large flat candle-stick, which I took outside and placed over the pipe, the candle-stick being placed shank downwards. This answered the purpose well enough so far as keeping the wind out, but at dark my room was filled with the choking smoke as bad as ever; the remedy was as bad as the disease. I had not calculated upon the smoke escaping. I had imagined that the wind getting into the pipe prevented the smoke getting out, consequently my plan was to adopt some method to keep the wind out, which I did most effectually. The sequel is known. Thus a man may acquire knowledge, piece by piece, and in some things become very clever, but notwithstanding may become entangled in his ideas with the simplest thing imaginable. Cleverer and wiser men than Mahommah, have done even more foolish things than this.

After this I returned to McGrawville for a short time, when, having a desire to see the manners and customs of the people living under the Government of Queen Victoria, of whom I had hoard so much, induced me to go to Canada, where I remained a short time, and being so well pleased with the reception I there met with, I at once determined to become a subject of her Majesty, for which purpose I attended at the proper office, gave the oath of allegiance, and procured my papers of naturalization without any difficulty.

I was kindly treated by all classes wherever I went, and must say in my heart I never expected to receive in a nation so distant from my native home, so much kindness, attention and humanity. I am thankful to God that I enjoy the blessings of liberty, in peace and tranquility, and that I am now in a land where "none dare make me afraid," where every man can or may "sit down under his own vine, and under his own fig tree:" where every man acting as a man, no matter what his color, is regarded as a brother, and where all are equally free to do and to say.

Being thus surrounded by friends, and enabled to enjoy the blessing of peaceful freedom, I came to the conclusion that the time had arrived when I might with propriety commit to paper all that has been recounted in this work, and whenever the day may come that a way may be opened to me of being useful in the regeneration of my own loved country, I shall be ready to say "I come," and may God in his infinite wisdom hasten that day, is the constant and fervent prayer of the subscriber, whose sufferings and tortures it is to be hoped have still further opened the ears and hearts of sensibility.

Should a call be given him to return once more to the land of his birth, he will cheerfully respond, and is sure friends will not be wanting to aid him in his benevolent purpose.

MAHOMMAH GARDO BAQUAQUA.

PRAYER OF THE OPPRESSED

Oh great Jehovah God of love.
Thou monarch of the earth and sky,
Canst thou from thy great throne
above
Look down with an unpitying eye

See Afric's sons and daughters toil,
Day after day, year after year.
Upon this blood-bemoistened soil.
And to their cries turn a deaf ear!

Canst thou the white oppressor bless
With verdant hills and fruitful
plains,
Regardless of the slave's distress
Unmindful of the black man's chains

How long oh Lord! ere thou wilt
speak
In thy Almighty thundering voice,
To bid the oppressor's fetters break,
And Ethopia's sons rejoice.

How long shall Slavery's iron grip.
And Prejudice's guilty hand,
Send forth, like blood-hounds from

the slip.
Foul persecutions o'er the land?

How long shall puny mortals dare
To violate thy just decree,
And force their fellow-men to wear
The galling chain on land and sea?

Hasten, oh Lord! the glorious time
When everywhere beneath the skies
From every land and every clime,
Peans to Liberty shall rise!

When the bright sun of liberty
Shall shine o'er each despotic land,
And all mankind, from boudage
free,
Adore the wonders of thy hand.